Primary Listening

20 Tips for Better Communication

Atsuko Tsuda

KINSEIDO

Kinseido Publishing Co., Ltd.
3-21 Kanda Jimbo-cho, Chiyoda-ku,
Tokyo 101-0051, Japan

Copyright © 2003 by Atsuko Tsuda

All rights reserved. No part of this publication may be reproduced, stored in a retrieval system, or transmitted, in any form or by any means, electronic, mechanical, photocopying, recording or otherwise, without the prior permission of the publisher.

First published 2003 by Kinseido Publishing Co., Ltd.

写真提供
p. 11, © Kongoji Ken / APL
p. 23, © Bill Bachmann / APL
p. 40, © JTB Photo
p. 42, © Yoshida Takashi / APL

装画　杉村早苗

はしがき

　文字で表されていれば、かなり高度な内容の英語でも理解することができるのに、耳から入ってくる英語に関しては単純な内容でもなかなか聞き取れないという学習者が日本人には多いように思われます。「リスニングのコツ、勉強法を教えてください」という相談も後を絶ちません。

　本書では、TOEIC、TOEFLのような検定試験をも念頭に置き、リスニングの目的とは何か、自分の弱点はどこにあり、それをどのようにして補うことが必要なのかを理解し、着実にリスニングの力を向上させていくことができるよう、多方面からリスニング力強化のポイントを示しています。具体的には、

　1. 普通のスピードで行われる日常的な話題の会話を理解することができる
　2. モノローグや、簡単なニュースを聞き取ることができる

ことを大きな目標とし、学習者にとってすぐに役立つように、トピックも海外旅行や外国人に日本を紹介する場面などを厳選しました。

　以下に各セクションの目的を記しますので、趣旨をご理解いただき、本書を活用していただきたいと思います。

- 聞き取りのポイント：英語の聞き取りにおいて注意したいことや問題点に焦点をあて、効果的な学習法、基本となるストラテジーを解説しています。
- Model Dialogues/Monologues/News：各ユニットのトピックに沿った内容の英文を聞き、聞き取りのポイントを確認しながら、耳から入る英語の特徴について学んでください。
- Exercises：各ユニットの聞き取りのポイントを再確認し、理解力を高めていくことができるよう、さまざまな練習問題を用意しました。
- Let's Challenge!：実際のコミュニケーションの場面に、本書で示されたリスニングストラテジーを応用する力がついているかどうか試してみましょう。

　本書で学習しながら、英語のリズム、スピードに慣れ、文法力や語彙、背景知識を強化すると同時に、記憶力、推察力を高めていく方法を身につけ、総合的にリスニング力をアップしていってくだされればうれしく思います。

　最後になりましたが、本書の作成にあたりお力添えいただいた金星堂編集部の諸氏、ならびに校正の段階で貴重なアドバイスをいただいた Ms. Carolyn Miller に心よりお礼申し上げます。

2003年1月　著　者

CONTENTS

UNIT 1   GOING THROUGH IMMIGRATION AND CUSTOMS *6*
センテンス・ストレス　内容語

UNIT 2   GETTING AROUND *8*
センテンス・ストレス　機能語

UNIT 3   STAYING AT A HOTEL *10*
場面設定と主題の理解

UNIT 4   AT A RESTAURANT *12*
話の展開の予測

UNIT 5   MAILING *14*
イントネーション

UNIT 6   SHOPPING *16*
数字（1）

UNIT 7   EXCHANGING MONEY *18*
数字（2）

UNIT 8   IN CASE OF TROUBLE *20*
疑問文の形をした表現

UNIT 9   RENTING A CAR *22*
音声の変化（1）

UNIT 10   COMMUNICATING WITH AIRLINE COMPANIES *24*
音声の変化（2）

UNIT 11   GEOGRAPHY *26*
数字（3）

UNIT 12   PEOPLE *28*
ポーズと意味のまとまり（sense group）
文頭からの理解

UNIT 13	SEASONS	30
	トランジションと内容の予測	
UNIT 14	FOOD	32
	文脈からの意味の推測	
UNIT 15	LANGUAGE AND LITERATURE	34
	事実と主観的見解の聞き分け	
UNIT 16	CUSTOMS	36
	指示対象の理解	
UNIT 17	TRADITIONS	38
	背景知識の活用	
UNIT 18	HOLIDAYS AND ANNUAL EVENTS	40
	リテンション	
UNIT 19	LISTENING TO MONOLOGUES	42
	情報の選択	
UNIT 20	UNDERSTANDING THE NEWS	44
	5Ws・1Hの聞き取り	
	内容語と背景知識の活用	

付属CDについて

巻末に付属しているCDには、本書のModel Dialogues/Monologues/Newsと各練習問題が収録されています(Let's Challenge! の問題はカセットテープのみ収録)。各問題ごとに頭出しができるようになっていますので、繰り返し聞いて理解を深めてください。

UNIT 1   GOING THROUGH IMMIGRATION AND CUSTOMS

聞き取りのポイント：センテンス・ストレス　内容語

英語の母音や子音、単語の発音に関する知識も大切ではありますが、実際のコミュニケーションは、基本的にフレーズ（句）、またはセンテンス（文）のレベルで行われるわけですから、まずは英語を聞いたときどのように聞こえてくるのかに慣れることが大切です。通常英語の文章でストレスがおかれる、すなわち強く発音される音節は内容語と呼ばれる単語にあります。内容語はそれ自体に意味を持つもので、聞き取りにおけるキーワードになっていくものです。名詞、動詞（be, do, 所有の意味を表す have を除く）、形容詞、指示代名詞、副詞、否定語、疑問詞などが内容語となります。聞き取りにくい箇所にこだわらず、まずは耳に強く残った単語をつなぎ合わせ意味を想像、理解するよう努めましょう。

MODEL DIALOGUES

Scene 1

A: May I see your passport, please?
B: Sure, here it is.
A: What's the purpose of your trip?
B: Sightseeing.
A: And how long are you planning to stay?
B: Five days.

Scene 2

A: Put your bags on this table, please. Your Customs form?
B: Here you are.
A: Thank you. Do you have anything to declare?
B: No.
A: Any meat, fresh fruit, or plants?
B: No.
A: Are you bringing any gifts into the country?
B: No.
A: Okay. Please give your form to that officer by the exit.
B: Thank you.

Scene 3

A: Could you tell me where the baggage claim counter is?
B: Yes, it's downstairs. Go straight to the end of the hall, and take the escalator to the first floor. It'll be right behind you when you get there.
A: I see. Thank you very much.
B: You're welcome.

1 次の文章の中で、ストレスが置かれる語（内容語）を○で囲み、実際の発音と比べ答を確認してみましょう。　**CD 4**

(1) Could I see your passport?
(2) Where are you staying?
(3) How long are you going to stay in the country?
(4) Is this your first visit?
(5) Are you here on vacation?
(6) Do you have any fruits or plants?
(7) Can you open your suitcase?
(8) What is in the bottle?

2 英文を聞き、文頭から耳に残った単語を書き取り、それぞれの文全体の意味を考えてください。　**CD 5**

Example : Which　　　hotel　　　staying
意味：どこのホテルに滞在するのか

(1) _____
　　意味：
(2) _____
　　意味：
(3) _____
　　意味：
(4) _____
　　意味：
(5) _____
　　意味：

Let's Challenge!　　会話を聞いて、文中の空所に適語を記入していきましょう。

A: Are you here on (　　　　)?
B: Yes.
A: Are they your (　　　　)?
B: That's right.
A: (　　　　) (　　　　) are you (　　　　)?
B: For a week.
A: Do you have any (　　　　) or (　　　　)?
B: No.
A: (　　　　) are these?
B: These are gifts for my friends here.
A: All right. Do you have any other (　　　　)?
B: No, we don't.
A: Fine. Here's your (　　　　).
B: Thank you.

UNIT 2　　　GETTING AROUND

聞き取りのポイント：センテンス・ストレス　機能語

英語の文章で強勢を受け、内容理解の大きな手がかりになるのは内容語ですが、そのほかの単語は機能語と呼ばれ文法的な意味しか持っていません。これらの語は自然な発話においては弱勢となるため、聞き取りにくいものとなっています。冠詞、前置詞、人称代名詞、所有代名詞、関係代名詞、接続詞、助動詞が機能語の仲間です。ただし例外として、文末にくる機能語は強勢を受けることがあります。内容語の合間合間にどのような機能語が置かれているかを理解するためには、耳だけに頼らず文法的な知識を活用していきましょう。

MODEL DIALOGUES

Scene 1

A: Where can I find a taxi?
B: Go straight until you come to the end of this building and turn right. There's a taxi stand just around the corner.
C: Where to?
A: Ferris Hotel.
C: That's a new hotel downtown, right?
A: Yes, it is.

Scene 2

A: Does this bus go to University Street?
B: Yes. Put the exact change in the fare box and seat yourself. The bus will be leaving in 10 minutes.
A: Okay. And how long will it take to get there?
B: Probably around 20 minutes. The traffic is not so heavy at this time of the day.

Scene 3

A: How many trains to Chicago are there per day?
B: Three or four, depending on the day of the week.
A: Have you got a copy of the timetable?
B: Sure, here it is.
A: Thank you, and how much is a ticket?
B: Thirty-two fifty, one way, and sixty even for round trip.
A: Do I have to make a reservation in advance?
B: That's advisable.
A: All right. Thank you.

1. 次の文章の中で、弱勢となる機能語を○で囲み、実際の発音と比べ答を確認してみましょう。　CD 9

(1) Where is the railroad station?
(2) Is there a bus that goes to China Town?
(3) May I see a timetable?
(4) Where does this bus go to?
(5) Do I have to transfer?
(6) How much is it to downtown?
(7) Could you take me to Macy's and bring me back to the hotel?
(8) Turn right at the next stop sign and drop me in front of the library.

2. 与えられた内容語を参考に、次の各文の空所にどのような語が入るかを予測してください。その後それぞれの英文を聞いて答を確認してみましょう。　CD 10

(1) How long (　　　) (　　　) take (　　　) get there?
(2) Where (　　　) I get off?
(3) What time (　　　) (　　　) last bus (　　　) (　　　) airport leave?
(4) You (　　　) keep (　　　) change.
(5) I (　　　) (　　　) missed my train.

Let's Challenge!　　会話を聞いて、次の各質問に答えましょう。

(1) Where is Ken heading for?
(2) Has his seat been reserved in advance?
(3) Why should Ken keep the window closed?
(4) What is in the middle of the train?
(5) What does Ken ask the conductor to do for him?

UNIT 3　　　　　　　　　　　　　STAYING AT A HOTEL

聞き取りのポイント：場面設定と主題の理解

話の内容を正しく理解するためには、まず会話が行われている場所、状況、話し手の関係、主題といった基本的な要素を把握することが大切です。特に、話し手がどこにいて誰と話しているかが分かれば、会話のおおまかな内容を想像することができ、聞き取りの助けとなってくれるはずです。そのような状況を特定することのできるキーワードを聞き漏らさないようにしていきましょう。

MODEL DIALOGUES

CD 11–12

Scene 1

A: Good afternoon, Paradise Hotel.
B: Hello, I was wondering if you have a room for this weekend.
A: Single or double occupancy?
B: Single.
A: Let me check … yes, we do. It's $60 per night.
B: That'll be fine. Could you hold it for me? My name is Sakamoto.
A: Yes, I can hold it for you until 6 o'clock this evening with no obligation on your part.
B: Wonderful. Thank you.

Scene 2

A: Good afternoon. How may I help you?
B: I'd like you to find me a baby-sitter for tomorrow evening.
A: Sure, that should be no problem. Your name and room number please?
B: Watanabe in Room 1105.
A: And from what time to what time?
B: Six to nine, probably.
A: All right.
B: If there's any change, I will let you know. Shall I call you or come back to this concierge desk?
A: You can just dial our extension number.
B: All right. Thank you very much.
A: Thank you.

1 (1)〜(5)の話し手は誰かを考え、最もふさわしいと思われる答をa〜eの中から選び、その記号で答えてください。　CD 13

(1) (　　)　　　　　　　　**a.** A hotel receptionist
(2) (　　)　　　　　　　　**b.** A housekeeper
(3) (　　)　　　　　　　　**c.** A porter
(4) (　　)　　　　　　　　**d.** A concierge
(5) (　　)　　　　　　　　**e.** A hotel guest

2 短い会話を聞き、話し手の関係を表す答を選びましょう。ヒントとなったキーワードは何だったかについても答えられるようにしてください。　CD 14

(1) **a.** A guest and a hotel receptionist
　　b. A bellboy and a guest
(2) **a.** A concierge and a hotel guest
　　b. A guest and a house keeper
(3) **a.** A guest and a hotel receptionist
　　b. Two hotel guests

Let's Challenge!　　ホテルでの会話を聞いて、次の質問に答えてください。

(1) Who is the guest speaking to?
(2) What is the guest doing?
(3) How does the guest feel about the hotel?
(4) What request does the guest make?

UNIT 4   AT A RESTAURANT

聞き取りのポイント：話の展開の予測

日本語の場合と同様、ある程度その内容が決まっているやりとりにおいては、それぞれの場面、状況に応じた話の流れを事前に予測しておけば焦ることはありません。また、相手の質問に関しては、それが Yes/No で答えるものか、疑問詞に対しての答を求めているものなのかを判断し、特に疑問詞を用いた質問の場合は、「何を」聞かれたのか正確に理解することがキーポイントとなります。

MODEL DIALOGUES

CD 15-17

Scene 1
A: Pacific Beach Restaurant, Nancy speaking. May I help you?
B: Yes, I'd like to make a reservation for tomorrow evening.
A: Yes, and for how many?
B: Two.
A: All right, and what time?
B: Seven.
A: Sure. Could I have your name, please?

Scene 2
A: Are you ready to order?
B: Yes, I'd like the cheese burger.
A: All right. Anything to drink?
B: Coffee, please.
A: Sure. Would you like cream and sugar with your coffee?
B: Yes, please.

Scene 3
A: Can I bring you anything else?
B: No, thank you. Could we have the check, please?
A: Sure, I'll be right back.
B: Thanks.

1. レストランでの短い会話を聞き、話の流れからこの後に続くと予測することのできない文を選び、記号を○で囲んでください。　**CD 18**

(1) **a.** Is it for tonight?
   b. What time, sir?
   c. How many people?

(2) **a.** I'd like the salmon.
   b. The seafood here is really nice.
   c. Will it be all for you?

(3) **a.** I'm sorry. We don't have any apple pies today.
   b. All right. Would you like me to bring you the check, then?
   c. Shall I bring you a menu?

2. (1)～(10)の質問は、それぞれ客(Customer)がしているのか、レストランの従業員(Restaurant Employee)がしているのかを考え、最もふさわしいと思われる答をa～mの中から選び、その記号で答えましょう。　**CD 19**

(1) (　　) (2) (　　) (3) (　　) (4) (　　) (5) (　　)
(6) (　　) (7) (　　) (8) (　　) (9) (　　) (10) (　　)

a. On King Street, just across from the Winston Hotel.
b. I'll be eating here.　　**c.** It's 80 dollars altogether.
d. Sure, no problem.　　**e.** What do you have?
f. Medium, please.　　**g.** Until 10:30.
h. Clam chowder. It's really good.　**i.** Non-smoking, please.
j. I'm sorry. We're fully booked tonight.
k. That's too much.　　**l.** Just fine, thanks.
m. Yes, thank you.

Let's Challenge!　レストランで3人の女性が食事を注文しています。会話を聞いて、それぞれが注文したものを答えてください。

Mary　(　　　　　　　　　　　　　　　　　)
Jane　(　　　　　　　　　　　　　　　　　)
Linda　(　　　　　　　　　　　　　　　　　)

UNIT 5   MAILING

聞き取りのポイント：イントネーション

話し言葉には文字や句読点がありませんから、声の調子が大事な役割を果たしています。話し手の用いるイントネーションは、その意図や情報を知る大きな手がかりの1つとなります。イントネーションだけで質問文になったり、同じ文でも意味が変わってきたりしますから、注意して聞きましょう。一般的に平叙文、命令文、疑問詞で始まる疑問文、感嘆文、確認のために用いられる付加疑問は下降調といって尻下がりのイントネーションとなり、Yes/Noで答える疑問文、丁寧さを込めた命令や疑問詞で始まる疑問文、聞き返し、Yes/Noで答える疑問文と同様に用いられる付加疑問などには上昇調といって尻上がりのイントネーションが使われます。

MODEL DIALOGUES

CD 20–21

Scene 1

A: Air mail?
B: Yes. How long will it take to Japan?
A: Probably about a week.
B: Oh, then can you send it express?
A: Sure. Anything else?
B: No, that's all.
A: That'll be eight twenty.

Scene 2

A: I'd like to send this parcel to Japan.
B: What are the contents?
A: Mainly clothes.
B: Please put your name, address, the receiver's address and name, the contents, and the total value on this form.
A: What is this for?
B: It's a customs declaration form.
A: I see. And how long does it take to reach Japan by sea mail?
B: Usually four to six weeks.
A: Oh, that long?
B: Air mail is much quicker but also far more expensive.
A: Then, sea mail is fine.

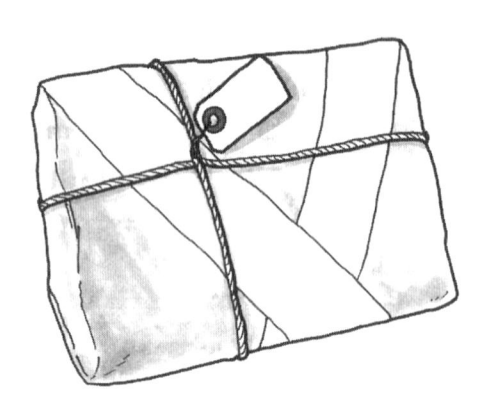

1. 次の英文を聞いて、そのイントネーションが上昇調か下降調かを聞き取り、話し手の意図として正しい方を選んでください。　　　CD 22

(1)　疑問　　　　　　　聞き返し
(2)　確認　　　　　　　疑問
(3)　通常の疑問　　　　丁寧な疑問
(4)　通常の疑問　　　　丁寧な疑問
(5)　発話の完結　　　　驚き

2. 短い会話を聞いて、次にあげた会話の抜粋部における話し手の意図に近い方の内容を表す文を選び、その記号を○で囲んでください。なお、抜粋部には句読点が含まれていません。　　　CD 23

(1) "The post office is near here, isn't it"
   a. I'm sure the post office is close from here.
   b. Is there a post office near here?
(2) "Oh, really"
   a. I don't care about the cost.
   b. I'm surprised to hear that.
(3) "What do I need"
   a. What do you want me to do?
   b. What kind of change do I have to have?
(4) "Sorry"
   a. Could you say that again?
   b. Please forgive me.

Let's Challenge!　次の日本語の文章の意味に沿って、イントネーションに気をつけながら英語で言ってみましょう。

(1) 葉書を5枚ください。
(2) これを私の代わりに出してくださいますか？
(3) 郵便局は何時に閉まるんですって？
(4) 私に手紙は来ていますか？
(5) 日本へファックスをしたいのですが。

UNIT 6　　　　　　　　　　　　　　　　　　　　SHOPPING

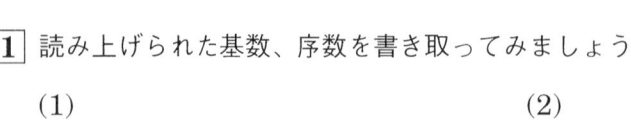

聞き取りのポイント：数字（１）

数字の聞き取りを苦手とする人は少なくありません。しかしどんなにシンプルな数字でも、聞き違えると困ったことになる場合がありますから絶対に慣れておきたいものです。まずは日常生活で頻繁に使用される基数、序数、ならびに時間、金額などが聞き取れるようにしましょう。　基数に関しては、少なくとも 1000 の単位まで特に 13 と 30、14 と 40 などの違いに注意して聞き取れるようにし、序数は 100 まで、時間、金額は数字の聞き取りのほかに、そういった表現の仕方、イントネーションを学んでください。

MODEL DIALOGUES

Scene 1
A: May I help you?
B: I'm looking for a swim suit. Where can I find one?
A: On the second floor, next to the women's casual wear section.
B: Okay. And what are your business hours?
A: From 10 to 9 on weekdays. And we close at 5 on weekends.
B: Thanks.

Scene 2
A: Can I try these pants on?
B: Of course. The fitting room is just behind the cashier over there.
A: Thank you.
B: How do you like them?
A: They're a little too big for me. Have you got a smaller size?
B: I'll check. What size do you have now?
A: Six.
B: I'll bring sizes 4 and 2 if we have any left.
A: Thanks.

Scene 3
A: I'll take this pair of shoes.
B: All right. Will that be all for you today?
A: Yes, I think so.
B: This way please. Cash or charge?
A: Can I use this credit card?
B: Sure, no problem. That'll be 65 dollars and 90 cents.

1 読み上げられた基数、序数を書き取ってみましょう。

(1)　　　　　　　　　　(2)
(3)　　　　　　　　　　(4)
(5)　　　　　　　　　　(6)
(7)　　　　　　　　　　(8)

2 読み上げられた時間、金額を聞き、答を○で囲んでください。　　　CD 28

(1)　7：15　　　　　　　　　　7：50
(2)　2：50　　　　　　　　　　3：10
(3)　11：30　　　　　　　　　 12：30
(4)　6：12　　　　　　　　　　6：20
(5)　4 dollars and 75 cents　　4 dollars and 70 cents
(6)　718 dollars　　　　　　　 7 dollars and 18 cents
(7)　1 dollar and 50 cents　　　50 cents
(8)　9,205 dollars　　　　　　　92,005 dollars

Let's Challenge!　　会話を聞き、空所に数字を記入していきましょう。

A: Where can I find children's clothes?
B: On the (　　　) floor.
A: I'm looking for some clothes for boys.
B: What age?
A: Actually, (　　　) and (　　　).
B: For boys above age (　　　), we have quite a good selection near the cashier. Turn right at the (　　　) aisle and you'll find them.
A: All right. And for younger ones?
B: We don't carry that much for toddlers. But we do have sizes (　　　) to (　　　) before the elevator.
A: Thanks. And how late are you open today?
B: Until (　　　).
A: Oh, no. I only have (　　　) minutes left.
B: Actually there is a good clothes shop for children not so far away from here at (　　　) Gerry Street. They are usually open till (　　　) or (　　　).
A: Oh, that's good to know. What's the name of the shop?
B: I think it's Kids & Kids.
A: What do you think is the best way to get there?
B: You can walk, but taking a cab might be easier. It's probably less than (　　　) minutes and will cost you somewhere between (　　　) and (　　　) dollars.
A: Thanks. By the way, how much is this pair of shoes?
B: Usually (　　　), but these are on sale now, so (　　　).
A: That's a good bargain.

UNIT 7   EXCHANGING MONEY

聞き取りのポイント：数字（2）

日常的に必要となる数字には、電話番号や両替の際の金額や紙幣の種類、枚数を表す表現などもあります。電話番号は、数字を1つ1つ読み上げますからさほど難しい聞き取りではありません。ただし、ゼロを"Oh"、下2桁が00で終わる場合、下三桁が000となる場合に、それぞれ"… hundred""… thousand"、また、同じ数字が続く場合に"double …"と言うことがあるので注意します。通貨の単位、また特にアメリカの硬貨の通称（penny, nickel, quarter）は知っておかなければなりません。紙幣に関しては、アメリカの場合1，5，10，20，50，100ドル札、イギリスでは5，10，20，50ポンド札があります。正式には、"… dollar / pound bill / note"と表されますが、金額を表す数字がそれぞれの紙幣の名前として用いられることが多い（たとえば"ten"は10ドルまたは10ポンド紙幣の意味）ので慣れておきましょう。

MODEL DIALOGUES

Scene 1

A: Excuse me. Where can I exchange money?
B: You can do that at the hotel reception desk or at a nearby bank. They might have better rates at a bank though.
A: Oh, I see. Do you happen to have the bank's phone number?
B: Let me see … Oh, yes. Here it is. 332-8154.
A: Let me repeat that. 332-8154?
B: That's right.
A: Thanks.

Scene 2

A: I'd like to exchange yen to dollars, please. What's the rate today?
B: One hundred and twelve yen to a dollar.
A: Then I'd like to exchange thirty thousand yen to dollars now.
B: Sure.
A: May I have a receipt, too?
B: Of course. Here you are.

Scene 3

A: Could you break a hundred-dollar bill?
B: Sure. How would you like it?
A: Three twenties, and the rest in ten dollar bills.
B: Oh, I'm sorry. I only have two twenty-dollar bills with me.
A: That's fine. Two twenties, and the rest in tens then.

1 読み上げられた電話番号、金額、硬貨や紙幣の種類や数量を表すものを a～e の中から選び、その記号で答えてください。　　　CD 32

(1) (　　)
(2) (　　)
(3) (　　)
(4) (　　)
(5) (　　)

a. 415-231-5907
b. 3 five dollar bills
c. 211-0068
d. 50 dollars
e. 60 cents

2 短い会話を聞き、それぞれの質問の答を完成させてください。　　　CD 33

(1) What is the new telephone number for the Bank of America?
　　It is _____.
(2) How many coins is the first speaker given?
　　He is given _____ 25 cent coins, _____ 10 cent coins and _____ 5 cent coins.
(3) How does the store's rate compare with the money changer's rate?
　　It is _____ yen higher than the money changer's.

Let's Challenge!　　Tomoko は銀行に来ています。会話を聞いて、次の各文の内容が会話の内容と一致していれば TRUE、異なっていれば FALSE を○で囲んでください。FALSE の場合は本文の内容に一致するように訂正してみましょう。

(1) Tomoko wants some traveler's checks.
　　　　　　　　　　　　　　　　　　　　　　　TRUE　FALSE

(2) She knew what an "ID" is.
　　　　　　　　　　　　　　　　　　　　　　　TRUE　FALSE

(3) She shows her passport to the teller.
　　　　　　　　　　　　　　　　　　　　　　　TRUE　FALSE

(4) She wants two hundred-dollar notes.
　　　　　　　　　　　　　　　　　　　　　　　TRUE　FALSE

(5) She did not understand the word "denomination".
　　　　　　　　　　　　　　　　　　　　　　　TRUE　FALSE

(6) She needs to pay a one percent service charge.
　　　　　　　　　　　　　　　　　　　　　　　TRUE　FALSE

UNIT 8　　　IN CASE OF TROUBLE

聞き取りのポイント：疑問文の形をした表現

日常会話では、一見疑問文のように見えますが、実際は「～してくださいますか」の意味の依頼や、「～はいかがですか」のような勧誘、提案、「～してもよいですか」と相手の許可を得るための表現が多く使われます。そのほとんどが、相手に対しての丁寧さを表すものですが、そのような表現と疑問文とをきちんと分けて理解できるようにしましょう。注意したい表現の例をいくつか挙げると以下のようになります。

Would/Could/Will/Can you …?
Would/Do you mind …?
May/Could/Can I …?
Would you like …?
Why don't you …?

MODEL DIALOGUES　　　CD 34-35

Scene 1

A: I left my bag in the taxi.
B: What kind of bag is it?
A: It's a black leather bag with a name tag on it.
B: What's in it?
A: A camera and my extra clothes.
B: We'll call you if we find it. Can you fill out this form and write down your contact address here?
A: Okay.
B: How long will you be staying in the city?
A: Until Friday.

Scene 2

A: What seems to be your problem?
B: I have a fever and a pain in my stomach.
A: How long have you had such symptoms?
B: The last two days.
A: Have you taken anything for your fever or stomachache?
B: No, nothing at all.
A: There's a bad virus going around and that's probably what it is, but let me examine you first. Are you insured?
B: Yes, I have travel insurance.
A: All right. Why don't you lie down there?
B: Okay.

1. 次の英文を聞き、それに対する応答としてふさわしいものを選び、その記号を○で囲んでください。
   CD 36

   (1) **a.** No, I couldn't.　　　　　　　**b.** I am sorry but I can't.
   (2) **a.** All right. Thank you.　　　　**b.** Because I don't feel like it.
   (3) **a.** Not at all.　　　　　　　　　**b.** Yes, I do.
   (4) **a.** I'm just looking, thanks.　　**b.** Of course not.
   (5) **a.** No, I wouldn't.　　　　　　　**b.** Yes, please.

2. 会話を聞き、空所に疑問文または依頼、提案などの表現を書き取り、会話を完成させてください。
   CD 37

   (1)
   A: Excuse me. I left the room key in my room. I'm locked out.
   B: Oh, (　　　) (　　　) (　　　) (　　　)?
   A: Room 255.
   B: And (　　　) (　　　) (　　　) (　　　) (　　　), (　　　)?
   A: Tanaka. Akiko Tanaka.
   B: All right. I will have someone bring the master key right away.
   　 (　　　) (　　　) (　　　) (　　　) (　　　) (　　　) (　　　) (　　　)?
   A: Thank you.

   (2)
   A: (　　　) (　　　) (　　　) (　　　) (　　　)?
   B: The air-conditioner in my room doesn't seem to be working.
   A: (　　　) (　　　) (　　　) (　　　) (　　　)?
   B: It makes a lot of noise and it doesn't get cool in the room.
   A: Mmm … that sounds strange.
   B: (　　　) (　　　) (　　　) (　　　) (　　　) (　　　) (　　　)?
   A: Right away. I'm sorry for the inconvenience.

Let's Challenge!　英文を聞き、それぞれの日本語の意味をa～eの中から選び、その記号で答えてください。

(1) (　　)　**a.** 白ワインは好きですか？
(2) (　　)　**b.** もう少し白ワインを召し上がりますか？
(3) (　　)　**c.** 白ワインはいかがですか？
(4) (　　)　**d.** もう少し白ワインをいただけますか？
(5) (　　)　**e.** どこで白ワインを買うことができますか？

21

UNIT 9　　　　　　　　　　　　RENTING A CAR

聞き取りのポイント：音声の変化（１）
自然なスピードで話される英語では、ある語の最後の音が次の語の出だしの音につながって発音されることがあります。このような現象を連結（リエゾン）と呼ばれますが、１つのまとまった意味を表す単語のまとまり（sense group）の中で起こります。同音が続いたときや以下のような音のつながりに注意して聞きましょう。

[r] + 母音	[z] + 母音	[p] + 子音
[n] + 母音	[tʃ] + 母音	[b] + 子音
[d] + 母音	[l] + 母音	[t] + 子音
[t] + 母音	[m] + 母音	[d] + 子音
[k] + 母音	[p] + 母音	[k] + 子音
[g] + 母音	[θ] + 母音	[g] + 子音
[f] + 母音	[s] + 母音	
[v] + 母音		

MODEL DIALOGUES

CD 38-39

Scene 1

A: Hi, may I help you?
B: Yes, I reserved a car and I'd like to pick it up. My name is Furuya, F-U-R-U-Y-A.
A: One moment, please. Yes, here we are. I need your driver's license, please. Did you want any extra insurance on it?
B: I don't know. What does it cover?
A: For example, in case of personal accident, medical expenses up to $2,000 for the driver and each passenger.
B: Mmm ... No, I don't think it'll be necessary.
A: All right, here's your rental agreement. Could you just sign here, and put your initials in two places on the form. Will that be cash or charge?
B: Charge. Do you take Visa?
A: Yes, we do.

Scene 2

A: Okay, you are all set. Do you have any questions?
B: Could you tell me what I should do in case of trouble?
A: Well, I'm sure you won't have any problems with our car, but if something should happen, just call this number. Someone is available 24 hours a day. And in case of accident, you are expected to notify the police immediately. The following procedures are all written at the bottom of the agreement.
B: All right. Thanks.
A: Not at all.

1 次の英文を聞き、それぞれの空所を補充して文を完成させてください。　CD 40

(1) We'll have your car ready (　　　) (　　　) (　　　).
(2) What (　　　) (　　　) (　　　) do you have?
(3) I think it's a (　　　) (　　　) to have full insurance.
(4) Please (　　　) (　　　) this form.
(5) May I see the car before I (　　　) (　　　)?
(6) Here's your contract. Please (　　　) (　　　) (　　　) carefully.

2 短い会話を聞き、次の質問に答えてください。　CD 41

(1) Is the car rental area far away from the office?
(2) How do you get to the car rental area?
(3) When is the customer expected to return the car?
(4) Where should the customer leave the car key?
(5) What does the customer ask for?

Let's Challenge!　音の連結を確認しながら、以下の英文を実際に発音してみましょう。

(1) Where can I rent a car?
(2) What is the drop off charge?
(3) How can I turn on the car radio?
(4) Please buckle up whenever you drive.
(5) Watch out! There is a car coming.
(6) I think this Toyota is the best deal. I'll take it.

UNIT 10　COMMUNICATING WITH AIRLINE COMPANIES

聞き取りのポイント：音声の変化（2）

いつでも相手が意識してゆっくりと話してくれるとは限りません。機能語の発音のされ方や、ネイティブスピーカーの "fast and relaxed pronunciation"（速度が早くくだけた発音）にも慣れておきましょう。

	Relaxed pronunciation
for	fer
to	ta
of	a
he/him/his/her	'e/'is/'im/'er
should/could/must etc. + have	shouda/coulda/musta
want to	wanna
going to	gonna
have to/has to	hafta/hasta
[t] + you/your	cha/cher
[d] + you/your	ja/jer

MODEL DIALOGUES

CD 42-43

Scene 1

A: Would you like a smoking or non-smoking seat?
B: Non-smoking, please. And I'd like to have an aisle seat if possible.
A: All right. Your seat is 24C. Please go to Gate 23 about 30 minutes before the boarding time.
B: Is the flight on schedule?
A: Yes, sir. Do you want to check in this bag?
B: Yes, please.

Scene 2

A: Excuse me, could you help us?
B: Sure. What can I do for you?
A: My friend cannot find his bag. He might have left it on the plane.
B: What does it look like?
A: It's a small brown bag.
B: And do you remember your seat number?
A: Yes. 25A.
B: I'm going to check. Could you wait here for a moment?

1　次の英文を聞き、それぞれの空所を補充して文を完成させてください。　CD 44

(1) (　　　　) (　　　　) tell me how (　　　　) fill in this form?

(2) What (　　　) (　　　　) like (　　　　　) drink?
(3) I (　　　　) (　　　　　) sit with my friend.
(4) Do I (　　　　) (　　　　　) check in this bag?
(5) Please come to the airport a couple (　　　　　) hours before the departing time.

2 会話を聞き、空所を補充して会話を完成させてください。　　　CD 45

A: I (　　　) (　　　　) change my flight. When is the next flight to Los Angeles (　　　　) (　　　　) leave?
B: We have two flights tomorrow, but our morning flight is full.
A: What time will the other one leave?
B: Three-thirty in the afternoon.
A: That'll be fine. (　　　　) (　　　　　) reserve an economy seat for me?
B: Sure. (　　　　) (　　　　　) show me the ticket you have?
A: Here it is.
B: Thank you. Here's your ticket (　　　　　) tomorrow, flight number 51.
A: By what time will I (　　　　) (　　　　) check in?
B: We are (　　　　) (　　　　　) start check-in at least 90 minutes before the departure time.
A: All right. Thank you.

Let's Challenge!　　会話を聞き、その内容に沿うように空所を補充する答を選び、その記号を○で囲んでください。

(1) The woman is calling Northwest Airlines to (　　　　　) her flight.
   a. reserve
   b. reconfirm
(2) Her flight is scheduled on Saturday, (　　　　　).
   a. August 7th
   b. August 17th
(3) She has one (　　　　) class seat.
   a. economy
   b. business
(4) The flight is for (　　　　　).
   a. Tokyo
   b. Osaka
(5) The departure time is (　　　　　).
   a. 3:45 p.m.
   b. 4:15 p.m.

UNIT 11　　　　　　　　　　　　　　　　GEOGRAPHY

聞き取りのポイント：数字（3）

桁の大きな数字や分数などについても、基本的な単位の取り方、読み方を理解しておけば焦ることはありません。どんなに大きな数字でも、英語では一度に3桁ずつ読み上げていく方式を取りますから、0から999までの数字が聞き取れれば、後は文字で表したときカンマを用いる位置でそれぞれ何というかを理解すればよいのです。

兆	千億	百億	十億	億	千万	百万	十万	万	千	百	十	一
1,	0	0	0,	0	0	0,	0	0	0,	0	0	0
trillion			billion			million			thousand			

ただし、上記の表はアメリカでの読み方で、billion, trillion は、イギリスではそれぞれ thousand million, billion となることに注意してください。

分数は、日本語では分母を先に読みますが、英語では分子を先に基数で、次に分母を序数で読みます。また、1/2 (a half), 1/4 (a quarter), 3/4 (three quarters), 14/125 (fourteen over one hundred and twenty-five) などの特殊な分数に慣れておきましょう。

MODEL DIALOGUES

CD 46-47

Scene 1

A: Where is Japan located?

B: Well, it is located off the east coast of Asia. The country is about 3,000km or 1,860 miles long from tip to tip.

A: And how big is the country?

B: Japan's land area is about 378,000km^2. It is smaller than California and approximately the size of Montana in the United States.

A: Oh, really? That's amazing.

Scene 2

A: What is the geography of Japan like?

B: It can be best described as a mountainous country. About 70 percent of its land area is covered with mountains, and only 13 to 15 percent of the land accounts for plains.

A: How many islands are there?

B: There are four main islands, Honshu, Shikoku, Kyushu, and Hokkaido. However, the country is made up of nearly 7,000 islands, and smaller isles scattered around the main islands.

1 読み上げられた数字を書き取ってみましょう。　　　　　　　　　　CD 48

(1) 　　　　　　　　　　　　　　　(2)
(3) 　　　　　　　　　　　　　　　(4)
(5) 　　　　　　　　　　　　　　　(6)
(7) 　　　　　　　　　　　　　　　(8)

2 短い会話を聞き、空所に数字を書き入れ会話を完成させてください。　CD 49

(1)
A: What's the total land area of Japan?
B: It's (　　　　　) square miles.
A: How does it compare to other countries?
B: Japan is slightly larger than Italy but (　　　　　　) of the United States.

(2)
A: Could you tell me about the nation's capital, Tokyo? Where is it located?
B: It's on the Kanto Plain, on the Pacific side of central Honshu.
A: What's the city like?
B: Actually, there are (　　　　　) wards, (　　　　　) cities, (　　　　　) county and (　　　　　) island units in Tokyo Prefecture. The metropolitan area is probably one of the busiest places in the world.
A: So I heard.
B: It is crowded with more than (　　　　　) people living there, and it is also very expensive. But many people find the city quite attractive. Tokyo's got everything, and in many ways, it is truly the center of the country.

Let's Challenge!　　次の日本語を英語に変えて言ってみましょう。

(1) 日本では年間1,000以上の地震があります。
　　1923年の関東大震災 (the great Kanto Earthquake) では10万人以上の死者がでました。
(2) 130万以上の人口を抱える京都は関西地方に位置し、202の国宝 (national treasures) と1,684の重要文化財 (important cultural properties) を所有する歴史的な都市です。
(3) 富士山は3,776メートル、または1万2,388フィートでの高さで、日本人に最も愛されている山です。

UNIT 12   PEOPLE

聞き取りのポイント：ポーズと意味のまとまり（sense group）
　　　　　　　　文頭からの理解

文章が長くなれば話し手は当然息継ぎをしなくてはなりません。日本語同様、この音声上のポーズは、息が苦しいからとどこで入れても構わないというものではありません。人によって頻度の差はありますが、息継ぎの場所は構文上の区切り、意味のまとまり（sense/thought group）となっていますから、聞き取りにおいての重要な鍵を握っているといえるのです。また、リーディングについてもいえることですが、英文を日本語に置き換えることをせず、主語＋述語動詞＋目的語／補語＋時間、場所などを表す表現といった英語の語順のまま、文頭から意味を理解していく癖をつけることが大切です。

MODEL DIALOGUES

Scene 1

A: What are some characteristics of Japanese people?
B: Well, many foreigners seem to think that the Japanese are a group-oriented people.
A: What does that mean?
B: Having a strong sense of belonging to certain groups, like families, companies and schools, is essential, and Japanese people make a great effort to maintain good relationship with others.
A: Living together in harmony is a wonderful thing, but doesn't it lead to lack of individuality if emphasis tends to be placed more on groups?
B: I suppose it does. The Japanese do not like being different or having different opinions from other people, and that's why they tend to be non-committal when they have to say either yes or no.
A: How about young Japanese people? Are they the same?
B: I think they are more assertive and are likely to express their ideas much more openly compared to older generations. But they, too, give a lot of consideration to other people's feelings before they speak or act.

Scene 2

A: I heard a new expression in Japanese today. What's *giri*?
B: Well, the expression, *giri*, refers to a sense of obligation. It's a social concept that one has to help or do favors to those who have helped him before.
A: How does the concept influence the behaviors of Japanese people?
B: We feel that we will lose trust or support from others if we neglect the obligation or do not offer proper help as necessary. A person who is careful to meet all *giri* obligations is highly appreciated in our society.
A: So the concept of *giri* has long been an integral part of the Japanese lifestyle, right?
B: I suppose you can say that.

1. 次の英文を聞き、ポーズが入っている箇所にスラッシュ (/) を入れ、スラッシュの区切りごとに意味を確認してみましょう。　　　　CD 52

(1) Compared to Americans, the Japanese put much greater emphasis on seniority. The sempai-kohai, or junior-senior tie, is determined by the date of entrance into a particular organization, such as school and company. Those who are older tend to be automatically respected in Japanese society, but under such social concept, a person's ability is sometimes completely ignored.

(2) Traditionally, many people thought that a woman's place was in the home, but things have changed slowly but steadily for women in Japan. Female participation in the work force has been increasing, and a number of women are now doctors, lawyers, scientists, and presidents of companies. Many jobs that were once considered men's are now open to women, too. However, it is still difficult for a woman in Japan to reenter the work force if she leaves her job for marriage, childbirth, or child care.

2. 会話を聞き、ポーズがきたらそこまでの意味を考え、以下の訳文の空所を埋めましょう。
　　　　CD 53
A: 「単身赴任」の意味は何か？
B: 夫が　/　(　　　　　) 妻や子と (　　　　　)　/　仕事上の (　　　　　) から
A: (　　　　　)　/　家族は (　　　　　)？
B: 大きな (　　　　　) は　/　おそらく (　　　　　)
　　もし (　　　　　) が (　　　　　) や国内のほかの土地に行くことになれば　/　彼らは (　　　　　) 必要がある　/
　　新しい (　　　　　)　/　(　　　　　)　/　(　　　　　) に
　　多くの (　　　　　) は　/　この変化を (　　　　　) と考える　/　特に (　　　　　) においては
B: それは残念なことだ。心から (　　　　　)　/　日本の (　　　　　) 夫たちに

Let's Challenge!　　Jane が Masao と仕事について話しています。会話を聞いて、次の各文の内容が会話の内容と一致していればTRUE、異なっていればFALSEを○で囲んでください。FALSEの場合は本文の内容に一致するように訂正してみましょう。

(1) Masao never works after 6 o'clock in the evening.
　　　　　　　　　　　　　　　　　　　　　　　　　　TRUE　FALSE
(2) Masao thinks it is hard for him to leave work before his boss does.
　　　　　　　　　　　　　　　　　　　　　　　　　　TRUE　FALSE
(3) The Japanese government has not encouraged people to work less.
　　　　　　　　　　　　　　　　　　　　　　　　　　TRUE　FALSE
(4) The number of people who take both Saturdays and Sundays off has been increasing.
　　　　　　　　　　　　　　　　　　　　　　　　　　TRUE　FALSE
(5) Jane doesn't feel Masao should work less.
　　　　　　　　　　　　　　　　　　　　　　　　　　TRUE　FALSE

UNIT 13　　　　　　　　　　　　　　　　　　　　SEASONS

聞き取りのポイント：トランジションと内容の予測

ネイティブスピーカーは、話の論理的展開を明らかにし、聞き手や読み手の理解の手助けとなるような語、句を多く用います。これらはトランジション(transition/transitional signals)などと呼ばれ、「道路標識」のような役割をするものですが、以下のような基本的な語句とその使われ方を頭に入れておくと、話し手の意図や内容の予測がつきやすくなるはずです。ただし一語の接続詞や前置詞は機能語のため、文中では聞き取りにくいので注意が必要です。

付加情報を表す	and, also, in addition, moreover, besides
逆説を表す	but, however, although, nevertheless, yet, on the other hand, while
例を示す	for instance, for example, such as, like, including
原因・理由を述べる	because (of), since, due to, owing to, as a result of, thanks to
結果を表す	so, therefore, as a result, consequently
順番を表す	first, second, then, next, finally
言い換える	that is, in other words, in short
結論を導く	in conclusion, in short
新しい話題に入る	listen, now, by the way

MODEL DIALOGUES

CD 54–55

Scene 1

A: Did you know Sei Shonagon wrote in *Makurano Soshi* about Japanese seasons? She said that dawn is best in spring, night is best in summer, twilight is best in fall, and early morning is best in winter.

B: That sounds romantic. In short, what she wanted to say is each season has its own, different charm, right?

A: Yes, exactly.

B: By the way, who is Sei Shonagon?

A: Oh, she is a renowned female author from the 10th century.

Scene 2

A: What is *setsubun*?

B: Originally, it meant the day before the season changes. We have four seasons; therefore, setsubun occurs four times a year. But today, only the change from winter to spring is observed.

A: When is it?

B: The third or fourth of February. We throw beans, shouting "Oni wa soto, fuku wa uchi!"

A: What does that mean?

B: "Out with demons, in with good luck!" In addition, it is customary to eat the same number of beans as your age. For example, if you are twenty, you eat twenty beans.

A: Oh, no. What if you become forty?

1 会話を聞き、空所にトランジションを書き入れ文を完成させてください。 　CD 56

(1)
A: _____ , I heard that Japan has four distinct seasons.
B: Yes. Spring, summer, fall and winter.
A: Does the climate vary greatly from season to season?
B: In most parts of Japan, it does. Spring and fall are more comfortable _____ it is neither too hot nor too cold. It is usually very hot and humid during the summer season _____ it gets cold in winter. On the Japan Sea side, it snows quite heavily.
A: Oh, really?
B: Yeah, _____ we have to wear clothes of different materials and colors to match the season.

(2)
A: When do you think is the best season to visit Japan?
B: Oh, that's a difficult question. I suppose it really depends on what you want to do and to see. _____ many Japanese might say that the best season is spring _____ you can see cherry blossoms and trees covered in fresh green. _____ in autumn, people enjoy leaves changing colors.
A: Oh, that sounds fantastic.
B: Yeah. _____, the weather is fairly stable during these seasons, _____ you won't have to carry heavy coats or umbrellas.

2 英文を聞き、使われたトランジションを参考にこの後に続く内容を予測し、適当と思われる答の記号を◯で囲んでください。 　CD 57

(1) **a.** … it has four different seasons.
    b. … it is located in the middle latitudes.
(2) **a.** … there is no rainy season there.
    b. … the Sea of Japan coast is under heavy snow.
(3) **a.** … it helps plants and crops to grow.
    b. … people get tired of it.
(4) **a.** … they are not at all pleasant.
    b. … rains that they bring makes an invaluable contribution to Japan's water resources.

Let's Challenge!　　Masao と Tom が話しています。会話を聞き、その内容に沿って次の文の空所を補充し、各文を完成させてください。

(1) Tom can't get used to summer in Japan because _____ .

(2) Tom can't stand _____ of the Japanese summer.

(3) On the contrary, Tom enjoys _____ .

(4) Masao doesn't enjoy snow in Tokyo since _____ .

UNIT 14　　　　　　　　　　　　　　　　　　　　　　　　FOOD

聞き取りのポイント：文脈からの意味の推測

どんなに高度な英語力を身につけていたとしても、話の中に未知の単語が出てくる可能性はなくなりません。そのような時には、前後の文脈と文法的な知識を使ってその部分の意味を推測することが大切です。また、英語ではなるべく同じ単語を繰り返さず、同意語や類語、言い換え表現を多く用いる傾向にあります。知らない単語が出てきたからといって焦らず、だいたいこんな意味のことを言ったのだろうと大まかな見当がつけられるようにしましょう。どちらにしても、分からない箇所にこだわらず、聞き取れた部分から内容の理解に結びつけていくのが早道といえます。

MODEL DIALOGUES

CD 58-59

Scene 1

A: What is the typical diet of Japanese people?
B: Traditionally, rice, miso soup, and some dishes containing meat, fish and vegetables. But I think the Japanese, especially younger generations, eat more westernized food. Hamburgers, curry and rice, and spaghetti are very popular items. Fast food has also become very popular throughout the country.
A: So Japanese eating habits are really diversified?
B: Yes, very much so. To foreigners, typical Japanese dishes may be *sushi*, *tempura* and *sukiyaki*, but they are not something we eat every day. Rather, we eat a variety of foods, such as Western, Chinese, Italian as well as traditional Japanese foods.

Scene 2

A: How do you find Japanese food?
B: I quite like it. I have tried many new things since I came to Japan.
   I think Japanese food is healthy and treasures natural flavors.
A: Is there anything you cannot eat?
B: I cannot remember the Japanese name, but those fermented soybeans are awful.
A: You mean *Natto*?
B: Yeah, that's it. I can't stand the smell and stickiness.
A: Well, you are not the only one.

1 次の英文の空所に入る品詞を考え、文脈に適した意味を持つものをあげてみましょう。その後、実際にそれぞれの英文を聞き、自分が用意した答と比べてみてください。
　　　　　　　　　　　　　　　　　　　　　　　　　　　　　　　　　　　CD 60

(1) These dishes are prepared to (　　　　) sake.
(2) Japanese food has (　　　　) popular in many foreign countries.
(3) There are many restaurants that offer foreign (　　　　).
(4) All Japanese dishes are eaten with (　　　　) made of wood, bamboo, or plastic.
(5) At a coffeehouse, or *kissatten*, you can have coffee, tea, or other (　　　　) and some snacks.
(6) Tofu is considered (　　　　) because it has a lot of vegetable protein.

2 会話を聞きながら、太字部分の単語の意味を文脈から推測し、その意味を表す答を選んで記号を○で囲んでください。
　　　　　　　　　　　　　　　　　　　　　　　　　　　　　　　　　　　CD 61

(1)
A: Is rice still a **staple** food?
B: It is hard to say. Rice consumption has greatly decreased over the past three to four decades. Many people today have bread for breakfast and noodles for lunch, including myself. But at the same time, rice seems to be something special to a number of Japanese people, particularly the elderly. Some people have to eat rice at least once or twice a day.

staple　a. expensive
　　　　　b. main or necessary

(2)
A: What am I not supposed to do with chopsticks?
B: First of all, you should never **stick** them upright in a bowl of rice or pass food from chopsticks to chopsticks.
A: Why not?
B: Because they have associations with funeral practices in Japan.
A: Oh, I see.
B: It is also considered bad-mannered to poke food with chopsticks and to **circulate** over the plates of food on the table trying to decide which to eat.

stick　a. thrust　　　　　**circulate**　a. break
　　　　b. move　　　　　　　　　　　　b. move around

Let's Challenge!　海外の日本料理についての説明文を聞き、次の各表現の意味を前後関係から推察し、日本語にしてみましょう。

(1) "around the globe"
(2) "cuisine"
(3) "recipes"
(4) "reimported to Japan"
(5) "modified"
(6) "low in fat"

UNIT 15　　　LANGUAGE AND LITERATURE

聞き取りのポイント：事実と主観的見解の聞き分け

個人の意見を述べるときによく使われるのは "I (don't) think/believe ..." "In my opinion ..." "I would say ..." などの表現ですが、このように明らかなシグナルを用いなくても発話内容が話し手の主観的見解であることを示してくれる語句があります。形容詞、副詞、助動詞などは、その種類、文脈での現れ方によっては、事実を述べるのではなく、個人の意見、証明できるような事実ではなく、状況から判断したことがらなどを述べる際の手段となりますから、注意して聞き分けていくようにしましょう。

MODEL DIALOGUES

CD 62-63

Scene 1

A: Since I have been in Japan, I have noticed that you use different characters in writing.
B: Yeah, that's right. We use *kanji, hiragana, katakana* and sometimes *romaji*.
A: Reading and writing Japanese should be the toughest thing in the world! Anyway, how do you use different characters?
B: Many nouns are written in *kanji*, characters brought in from China. Adjectives are written mostly in *kanji-hiragana* combination. Other parts of speech such as particles and auxiliary verbs are written in *hiragana*, and loan words, or *gairaigo* are written in *katakana*.
A: Oh, no. I'll never be able to remember.

Scene 2

A: Have you ever read any Japanese novels?
B: Yes. The first one was Mishima's *The Temple of the Gold Pavilion*. I found it intriguing.
A: Did you read it in English?
B: Of course! A number of Japanese literary works have been translated into English. I also liked *The Makioka Sisters* very much.
A: *The Makioka Sisters*?
B: Oh, I think the Japanese title was *Sasame Yuki*. It's written by Junichiro Tanizaki.
A: Oh, yes! He is the greatest.

1　次の英文を聞き、空所を補充し文を完成させてください。その後、それぞれの文が事実を述べるものか、主観的な見解を表すものかを考えてください。　　CD 64

(1) Japanese is the (　　　　　) official language (　　　　　) in Japan.
(2) Japanese (　　　　　) be one of the (　　　　　) (　　　　　) languages to learn.
(3) *Tanka* is a (　　　　　) poetic form perfected in the beginning of the (　　　　　) century.
(4) The number of loan words has (　　　　　) in recent years.

(5) It is (　　　) to know that (　　　) and (　　　) students are taking Japanese classes overseas.
(6) (　　　), Arthur has lost his (　　　) in studying Japanese.
(7) I (　　　) the (　　　) record of Japanese dates back to the third century.
(8) Yukio Mishima is my (　　　) author.

2 会話を聞き、空所（1）〜（5）の台詞を聞き取り、その内容が事実を述べるものか、主観的な見解を表すものかを考えてください。　　　　　　　　　　　　　　　CD 65

A: Is it difficult to learn Japanese?
B: Well, (　　　1　　　).
   But (　　　2　　　).
A: What do you mean?
B: (　　　3　　　). If the person is older or has a higher social status, for example, you use special words to show respect or to show modesty.
A: (　　　4　　　).
B: Yeah, I know. But (　　　5　　　). Even native speakers of Japanese need some training and practice to use polite language properly.

(1) _____
(2) _____
(3) _____
(4) _____
(5) _____

Let's Challenge!　　俳句についての会話を聞き、次の中から会話の内容に沿わないもの、または出てこなかったものを選び、その記号を○で囲んでください。

Haiku　**a.** is not at all known outside Japan
　　　　b. is unique to Japan
　　　　c. the shortest poetic form in the world
　　　　d. is composed of three lines
　　　　e. is awfully difficult to translate into English
　　　　f. has 17 syllables in a 5-7-5 arrangement
　　　　g. needs to have a seasonal word
　　　　h. deals with life and nature
　　　　i. was established as an art by Matsuo Basho in the Edo period
　　　　j. is not as popular as before

UNIT 16   CUSTOMS

聞き取りのポイント：指示対象の理解

すでに話に出てきた名詞は、その後代名詞や the+ 名詞の形に置き換えられていきます。英語が文字で表されているとき、代名詞や the+ 名詞が何を指していたかは、文章の前に戻って目で確認することができますが、リスニングでは話の流れに沿って、それぞれの指示対象が何であったかを正確に判断する力が必要です。既出の名詞の種類や人称、どのような名詞に置き換えられるか（例えば、"Japan" であれば "the country/nation" などに変わる可能性がある）などに注意を払いながら聞きましょう。

MODEL DIALOGUES

CD 66-67

Scene 1

A: I have noticed that some gestures you use in Japan are the same as those in the United States.
B: Like what?
A: For example, you also draw a hand across your neck to mean "being fired."
B: Oh, that one.
A: Right. But Japanese gestures to mean "come here" and "money" were really confusing. It took me a while to understand the two.
B: Why did you find them confusing?
A: Well, Japanese "come here" looks similar to our "good bye" or "go away" and "money" with a circle with thumb and forefinger means "okay" to us.

Scene 2

A: I had my *hanko* made last week.
B: Wow! Let me take a look at it.
A: You see, my last name is carved in *katakana*.
B: Neat! But do you really need one?
A: Well, not really because I'm a foreigner. But I learned that Japanese people use *hanko* for legal and important documents instead of a signature. I thought I might as well have one made while I'm in Japan.
B: Have you used it yet?
A: Not yet. I hope to have a chance soon.

1 会話を聞き、太字部分がどのような表現に置き換えられていくかを確認しましょう。

CD 68

(1)
A: You know, there is **one Japanese custom I really love**?
B: What is it?
A: No tipping!
B: Yeah, that's true.
A: In **the States**, you have to give a tip everywhere you go.
B: Yes, I remember. I had to study **to whom, how and when, and about how much you have to leave a tip** before going to the country.

A: It's really nice that you don't have to worry about things like that.
B: I agree.

(2)
A: How do Japanese people feel about gift-giving practices?
B: You mean **chugen and seibo gifts**?
A: Yeah. What are they for anyway?
B: *Chugen* means mid-year and *seibo* means year-end. Twice a year, we show our appreciation, especially to those in socially superior positions, by sending **gifts**.
A: Do you send them, too?
B: Yes, to my boss, marriage mediator, and so on.
A: Sounds like **the custom** calls for a lot of money.
Twice a year, to a number of people, right?
B: Yeah. I think more and more people feel discontented with it because it's troublesome and costly. Many people realize that **gift-giving** has become obligatory, and some people say that we should do away with it altogether.

2 会話を聞き、次にあげた抜粋部の太字部分が何を指すかを考え、正しい答の記号を○で囲んでください。

CD 69

(1) "Do you know what **they** are?"
   a. Japanese businessmen
   b. small cards
(2) "I think **they** were exchanging *meishi* …"
   a. Japanese businessmen
   b. small cards
(3) "… to be able to read it when **he** receives it"
   a. the lower ranking or younger person
   b. the other person
(4) "**That** makes sense."
   a. the custom of exchanging name cards
   b. the rule about exchanging name cards

Let's Challenge!   Helen と Michiko が日本の習慣について話しています。会話を聞き、次の各質問に答えてください。

(1) What Japanese customs did Helen know before coming to Japan?
(2) What does Helen like better than her country's now?
(3) What did Helen do at a neighborhood bathhouse?
(4) How does Michiko describe *sento*?
(5) Which Japanese custom does Helen find difficult?
(6) What suggestions does Michiko give to Helen?

UNIT 17　　　　　　　　　　　　　　　　　　　TRADITIONS

聞き取りのポイント：背景知識の活用

リスニングというと耳に頼りすぎる人が多いのですが、残念ながら意味が分からない単語を何度繰り返し聞いても仕方ありません。前後関係や、文法的知識を駆使しておおよその見当をつけることが大切だということは先に述べましたが、英語を取り巻く文化や、話のテーマについての知識が理解度を大きく左右することも事実です。専門的な知識である必要はありませんが、可能な限り幅広い分野にわたり多くの知識を蓄えることで、内容の推測ができることが少なくありません。英語の勉強だけが、英語力のアップにつながるのではないということを覚えておきましょう。

MODEL DIALOGUES

CD 70-71

Scene 1

A: Do Japanese girls learn *ikebana* and tea ceremony at school?

B: Not really. Some schools have *ikebana* club and tea ceremony club. Interested students can engage in such extra curricular activities after school.

A: Are they really popular?

B: I think they still are. But modern Japanese girls have more diversified interests and wider selections. You know, until sometime ago, like in my grandmother's or my mother's time, young girls were expected to learn to perform such traditional arts as part of their training before marriage.

A: Oh, I see.

Scene 2

A: I'm really interested in *shodo*, you know, the art of calligraphy. I went to an exhibition the other day and became absolutely fascinated.

B: Writing Japanese with brush and ink is difficult for Japanese people too. You need some training and practice.

A: Have you ever done it?

B: Yes. First in elementary school, but I didn't continue. Then I thought I wanted to improve my handwriting and took some lessons for a while.

A: How was it?

B: It was good. You need to sit straight and compose yourself. You pay attention to the movement of your brush, the shades of the ink …. I think it is really a good way to cultivate your inner self.

1 次の各文の空所にはどのような情報が入るかを、背景知識を利用して予測してみましょう。その後、英文を聞き、それぞれの空所部分の内容を書き取ってみてください。　CD 72

(1) The art of *kabuki* acting _____ from father to son, and training starts from _____.

(2) In the tea ceremony, _____ are used. There are numerous rules in tea making procedures including _____.

(3) Bonsai are grasses and trees transplanted into small containers and grown into _____. _____ are required to create particularly aesthetic figures.

(4) Traditional Japanese gardens are composed of _____. They are designed to reflect the beauty of nature.

(5) *Bunraku* is _____ that is unique to Japan. The puppets are manipulated by three people in accordance with music and chants called *joruri*. They have little facial expression, but laugh, weep, and get angry as if _____.

2 「浮世絵」について知っていることを全て書き出してみましょう。(日本語でも英語でも構いません。) その後、浮世絵に関する英語の説明文を聞き、下の表の聞き取れた項目に情報を書き入れ完成させてください。　CD 73

　　浮世絵：　　背景知識

Definition	
Time	
Famous Artists	
Subjects	
Influence	

Let's Challenge!　英文を聞く前に、次の各質問に目を通し、背景知識を利用して答を予測できるものがあるかどうかチェックしましょう。その後、会話を聞きそれぞれの質問の答を確認してください。

(1) What three examples of traditional theater (伝統演劇) in Japan are mentioned?
(2) Which one is the oldest of the three?
(3) How is *noh* different from the other two?
(4) How is *noh* performed on a stage?
(5) How many categories are most *noh* plays grouped into?
(6) What influenced *noh*?

UNIT 18　　HOLIDAYS AND ANNUAL EVENTS

聞き取りのポイント：リテンション

ある程度英語のリスニングに慣れてくると、聞き取る力だけではなく、聞き取れなかった部分を様々な側面からどの程度まで補うことができるかが重要なポイントであることが分かってくるはずです。話の流れ、トピックを正確に把握し、背景知識や文法力など、自分の持っているものを総動員して内容理解に結びつけていけるようにしましょう。そういったことができているかを確認する１つの方法として、「リテンション」があります。これは、１回聞いた文章をメモなどを取らずにそのまま音声で繰り返すというものです。通訳訓練では記憶力の養成に用いられている方法ですが、自分の英語力、背景知識が高ければ高いほど、楽に行うことができるようになります。

MODEL DIALOGUES

Scene 1

A: Which one is the most significant national holiday in Japan?
B: Probably New Year's Day. Everything except some convenience stores, entertainment facilities and public transportation is closed.
A: Oh really? What do people do on that day?
B: Family members exchange formal greetings and celebrate the start of the new year by having special New Year's dishes. Many people also pay their first visit to a shrine or temple to pray for happiness, good health or prosperity.

Scene 2

A: Do you celebrate Christmas in Japan?
B: Probably not in the same way as you do. It's not so much of a religious event here.
A: What do people do?
B: For young couples, it's a romantic day to share with each other. Children, of course, love receiving presents from so-called "Santa Claus."
A: And for others?
B: Christmas is not necessarily a special occasion though you'll find a Christmas tree at every corner of the street and the town is filled with Christmas songs.

1 会話を聞き、空所部分(1)〜(3)の内容を正しく再現している文章を選びその記号を○で囲んでください。　　　　　　　　　　　　　　　　　　　　　　　CD 76

A: How many national holidays are there in Japan?
B: Fifteen by law. (　　　1　　　).
A: What does the law stipulate?
B: (　　　2　　　).
A: Oh, that's nice.
B: Yes, really. (　　　3　　　).

(1) **a.** But actually we have more because of the Happy Monday Law.
　　b. We have more holidays now because of the Monday Holiday Law.
(2) **a.** If a holiday happens to be on a Sunday, the next Monday substitutes for it.
　　b. When a holiday falls on a Sunday, the following Monday substitutes for it.
(3) **a.** We don't lose any national holidays and have more longer weekends that way.
　　b. We don't have to lose any national holidays and get more longer weekends that's why.

2 (1)〜(5)までの英文を聞き、耳から入った文章をそのまま声に出して言ってみましょう。その後、自分がどの部分を再現できなかったか、またその理由は何かを確かめてください。　　　　　　　　　　　　　　　　　　　　　　　　CD 77

(1)
(2)
(3)
(4)
(5)

Let's Challenge!　　会話を聞き、なるべく会話の中で使われた表現を用いて次の各質問の答を用意してください。

(1) Why do the Japanese love cherry blossoms so much?
(2) What is *hanami*?
(3) What do people do?
(4) Where do people go for *hanami*?

UNIT 19　　　　LISTENING TO MONOLOGUES

聞き取りのポイント：情報の選択

会話（dialogues）ではなく、話し手が相手なしに1人で話すのがモノローグ(monologues)と呼ばれるものです。アナウンスや録音されたメッセージなどがモノローグの例としてあげられますが、このような台詞はただ漠然と聞いていては大切な情報を聞き漏らしてしまいます。かといって一言一句聴き逃すまいとして身構える必要もありません。取捨選択し、その時に自分に取って必要な情報を確実に聞き取ることが最も重要です。話の流れの中で、「あ、ここからは自分にとって大切なことを言ってくれるぞ」という箇所に気づき、即座に反応できるようにしておきましょう。

SAMPLE MONOLOGUES

Monologue 1

Good evening. I'm Kathy, and I'll be serving you tonight. I'd like to explain our specials today. First of all, our soup of the day is Manhattan clam chowder. Our special appetizers today are fresh oysters and smoked salmon. Also for main dishes, we have grilled lamb with fresh herb sauce and sauted scallops tonight. I'll come back later to take your orders.

Monologue 2

Departing passengers on American Airlines Flight 052 for New York are now boarding. Please proceed to Gate Number 23. Also, this is a final call for Delta Airlines Flight 002 for Miami. All passengers are required to proceed to Gate 12 immediately. Thank you.

Monologue 3

Thank you for calling Sunshine Florist. We are open Monday through Thursday, 9 to 7, and Friday to Sunday, 10 to 5. Stop by this week and receive a free package of flower seeds with your purchase. Our trained staff will help you choose the best flowers for your special occasions.

1 英文を聞き、次の各質問に答えてください。　　　　　　　　　　　　　CD 81

(1) **a.** Where would you hear this announcement?
　　b. How long will the flight be?
　　c. Where can you put your bags besides overhead storage compartments?
　　d. What happens after dinner?

(2) **a.** What kind of movie is being shown at the theater?
　　b. How long is the movie?
　　c. What time does the last show begin?
　　d. How much is the admission fee for an adult?

2 英文を聞き、与えられた場面設定に合わせてそれぞれの質問に答えてください。
　　　　　　　　　　　　　　　　　　　　　　　　　　　　　　　　CD 82

(1) You are taking Delta Airlines Flight 401.
　　What do you have to do now?

(2) You have just gotten on eastbound Highway 30 to work.
　　a. How is the traffic on Highway 30?
　　b. What is the problem?
　　c. What can you do now?

Let's Challenge! 　　英文を聞き、以下の日本語訳文を、英語でアナウンスされた順番に並べ替えてください。

(1) ラスベガス行き、125便をご利用のお客様は、私どもの地上勤務員に乗り継ぎに関してお尋ねください。
(2) このたびはユナイテッド航空をご利用いただきありがとうございました。
(3) ハーディング機長ならびに乗務員一同、皆様のサンフランシスコでの滞在が快適なものであるようお祈りいたします。
(4) 途中予期せぬ乱気流発生のため到着時刻に20分の遅れがでましたことをお詫び申し上げます。
(5) 皆様、当機はまもなくサンフランシスコ国際空港に到着いたします。
(6) また近い将来、皆様に機内でお会いするのを楽しみにしております。

　　(　　)→(　　)→(　　)→(　　)→(　　)→(　　)

UNIT 20　　　UNDERSTANDING THE NEWS

聞き取りのポイント：５Ｗｓ・１Ｈの聞き取り
　　　　　　　　内容語と背景知識の活用

英語のニュースは、確かに最初は話すスピードが速く感じられ、聞き取りに苦労するかもしれませんが、言葉の面から考えると、何度も読み返すことのできる新聞や雑誌に比べ、放送英語の方が理解しやすいようにと考えられているとする人もいます。聞き取りに関しては、特に内容語に注意を払い、理解できた内容語からニュース全体の意味を推察するようにします。特に、ニュースの場合１つの文章に盛り込まれる内容が多くなりますから、5Ws (who, what, when, where, why) 1H (how)、つまり、主語、述語動詞、時間、場所、理由などを表す表現を、文頭から頭の中で整理しながら正しく理解できるようにする訓練が必要です。同時に、政治、経済、医療など様々な分野の話題、用語に対応できるよう、リスニング以外にも日頃からボキャブラリービルディングに努めましょう。また、日本語で聞いても分からないことは英語で理解できるわけがありませんから、背景知識を豊かにし、聞き取れなかった箇所をそういった知識で補うようにしていくことが大切です。

SAMPLE NEWS

CD 83-85

News Clip 1

According to the Energy Conservation Center, about 86 percent of Japanese households owned air conditioners in fiscal 2000.

News Clip 2

The Tokyo metropolitan government has decided to deposit more than 100 billion yen in public funds in Citibank this fiscal year to diversify risks. It will be the first local government to keep its public funds in a foreign bank.

News Clip 3

China invoked retaliatory measures against Japan for Tokyo's curb on Chinese imports. The measures are for motor vehicles, mobile telephones, and air conditioners. Affected industries are desperately calling for reconciliation by both governments.

1 ニュースを聞き、いくつかのキーワードを書取り、それぞれがどの分野の内容を伝えているかを考え、答をa～eの中から選び、その記号で答えてください。　　CD 86

(1) (　　) 　Key words:　　　　　　　　　　　**a.** 政治・外交
(2) (　　) 　Key words:　　　　　　　　　　　**b.** 経済・ビジネス
(3) (　　) 　Key words:　　　　　　　　　　　**c.** 医療・科学
(4) (　　) 　Key words:　　　　　　　　　　　**d.** 犯罪
(5) (　　) 　Key words:　　　　　　　　　　　**e.** 災害・事故

2 ニュースを聞いて、最初の文に関して次の表の該当項目を完成させてください。また、残りの部分からはどのような情報を得ることができたかを確認してみましょう。このトピックに関してどのような背景知識を持っていたかについても考えてみましょう。

CD 87

最初の文から得た情報：

誰が	who	
～をした	what	
いつ	when	
どこで	where	
なぜ	why	
どのように	how	

残りの部分から得た情報：

背景知識：

Let's Challenge! ニュースを聞いて、次の各質問の正しい答を選び、その記号を○で囲んでください。

(1) What is this news about?
   a. an accident
   b. a crime

(2) What happened?
   a. A man shot his gun.
   b. An emergency alarm went off, causing panic among passengers.

(3) Where did it happen?
   a. at the Los Angeles airport
   b. at an airport in Egypt

(4) How many people were killed or injured?
   a. Two people were killed and four were injured.
   b. Thousands of people were injured.

(5) How did the incident affect domestic flights?
   a. Most flights were delayed.
   b. It did not have any impact on domestic flights.

(6) Who conducted an investigation after the incident?
   a. FBI
   b. A 41-year-old resident of Irvine, California

本書にはカセットテープ(別売)があります

Primary Listening
―コミュニケーションのための基礎リスニング―

2003年1月20日 初版発行
2021年3月25日 重版発行

著 者 津 田 敦 子
発行者 福 岡 正 人
発行所 株式会社 金 星 堂
(〒101-0051) 東京都千代田区神田神保町 3-21
Tel. (03)3263-3828 (営業部)
　　 (03)3263-3997 (編集部)
Fax (03)3263-0716
http://www.kinsei-do.co.jp

印刷所／日新印刷　製本所／松島製本　1-11-3769
落丁・乱丁本はお取り替えいたします

ISBN978-4-7647-3769-3 C1082